Value Investing Fundamentals: Build a High-Performance Value Investing Portfolio

An Essential Guide to Investments: Capital Allocation, Position Sizing and Portfolio Management

Shailesh Kumar, MBA

Copyright © 2019 Shailesh Kumar
All rights reserved.

https://valuestockguide.com

PREAMBLE

So, you have learned how to analyze stocks and companies.

Congratulations!

What now?

There are many books that teach you the accounting principles. They also teach you how to calculate different ratios, find out the intrinsic value, determine the margin of safety, and figure out if a stock is a good value or not.

This book does not do any of these things.

Instead, it will show you how to use your knowledge in practice and build and operate a high performance, well oiled, value investing portfolio.

Without the practical wisdom, theoretical knowledge is useless.

In some situations, it can lose you money.

But we will fix that.

Let's begin.

CONTENTS

Preamble

Introduction

Principle 1: Investments Only Make Sense When There is a Better Than Even Chance of Profit

The Secret To Beating The Market By 6% Over The Long Term: Buy The Right Asset Class

Principle 2: Risk Management and Correct Position Sizing is One of the Key Drivers of Profits

How We Use The Volatility Based Risk Parity Method At Value Stock Guide To Size Positions Correctly And Manage risk?

Principle 3: Every Little Bit Matters. We Take All Measures Necessary To Improve The Odds Of Profit And Eliminate As Much Risk In The Portfolio That We Can

MYTH #1: Stock Markets are Efficient

MYTH #2: Mere Mortals Like You and I cannot Beat the Market

MYTH #3: Excessive Diversification Improves Returns and Reduces Risk

MYTH #4: Company Stock Buybacks Are Good

MYTH #5: We Should Avoid Stocks that are not very Liquid

Advice #1: Do NOT Use Beta of a Stock as Part of Your Investment Decisions

Advice #2: Investing Risk is Not What You Think It Is

Bonus #1: Value Investing – Why Do You Fail?

Bonus #2: Think Value Investing is Buy and Hold Investing? Think Again

Final Thoughts

About the Author

INTRODUCTION

Investing is closely related to Economics. Just like economics, investing is not all science. At its core, it is a study of how the market works in practice. Theory, therefore, is derived from observing the practical. Markets do not behave according to these theories, but rather, these theories adapt to the changing market behavior.

We start this book 3 principles that a value investor must follow to succeed in the market. This includes a discussion of the anomalies that the academics have not been able to explain. We look at the evidence/research that supports the existence of these anomalies over a period. You will learn how to take advantage of these anomalies by properly positioning your portfolio in the right asset classes.

The right asset class will over time deliver close to 6% extra return over the total stock market index.

Next, we consider the topic that is normally not covered in most books on value investing.

Arguably, position sizing and risk control are even more important than picking great stocks. Your long-term performance is greatly influenced by the money you *do not lose*. According to some, proper position sizing and risk control can make a random stock portfolio a market beating portfolio.

So why is this topic given such a scant attention in the literature?

Mainly because these concepts are borrowed from the world of day trading and blackjack tables in Vegas and we value investors have been slow to adapt. We are told to buy as much as we can when we find a great stock. But when you are buying 5 different stocks, this advice does not make much sense. What should the relative weights be for each of the stocks? How do we determine these weights?

I present one way to allocate capital in your portfolio that controls for risks inherent in each of the stock.

Then we systematically go down the list of 5 investing myths that I have found in my 20+ years of value investing practice to be not true. These are empirical observations on the market and my conclusions are what I have found to work. Several other value investors have lent support to these with their own experience, and of course, this explains the existence of super investors such as Warren Buffett and Benjamin Graham.

These are still the myths that continue to be perpetuated by the financial media. The result is that most investors now conform to the same set of advice on investing. The primary aim is helpful – but it is intended to ensure that you do not lose to the market. If we were to do better than the market, we need to actively find ways to increase our edge over the market.

Once you go through the 5 myths, and then read further advice on risk and risk management, you will be ready to learn about value investing. I have added 2 bonus articles on Value Investing to get you started.

In summary, this book will tell you,

1. Where you get the best odds of profitable ideas?
2. How much you should allocate to each of these ideas and how to control risk? and,
3. What kind of market noise you should ignore so you stick to your process?

Once you understand these concepts and adopt them in your investing practice, you should be able to do much better than 6% average annual profit in excess of the market returns, over a long term.

PRINCIPLE 1: INVESTMENTS ONLY MAKE SENSE WHEN THERE IS A BETTER THAN EVEN CHANCE OF PROFIT

Students of value investing all know the basic principles that were laid down by Ben Graham and other value investors who followed in his footsteps.
1. Find stocks with prices well below its intrinsic value
2. Buy the stock and wait for the market to correct its mistake, and,
3. When it does, profit handsomely

Let's examine these 3 points.

Find Stocks with Prices Well Below Its Intrinsic Value

Right away we see that we need to figure out the intrinsic value of a stock as soon as we start our due diligence. There are many ways to do this. You are aware of the most common method employed by the not very sophisticated investors – look for price multiples of earnings or book value or sales and if the ratio is lower than some benchmark (for example, the market P/E ratio, or the PE ratio of the peer group companies, or if there are no comparables, we may even compare the current P/E ratio with the company's historical values), then the stock is considered a great value.

This is a one approach fit all method that generally works. You are likely not going to get too many good opportunities if you use this method, since millions of other investors are using these very same methods, and many of them have significantly more money to invest than you do.

The other glaring problem with this is that it breaks down in many situations. These situations tend to be relatively rare, but boy oh boy, some of the juiciest values can be found in the anomalies in the market, and if you are looking for value using the multiples method, you will pass these anomalies right over and never see them.

Step 1: Start Your Research with Screens
Let me make something very clear. These screens are incredibly useful. They are the starting point for most systematic research process. The trick is to employ several screens of these sorts – P/E ratios, P/B ratios, Book Value Growth, etc. And then look for both extremes. For example, if you run a P/E multiple screen, I recommend you look for low P/E ratios (as is traditionally recommended) and

consider extremely high P/E ratios as these are the anomalies that you need to look deep into. If you need more help with screens, I provide extensive value stock screening criteria on my website for free

Step 2: Do A First Pass Research on The Shortlist of Stocks and Put Them In Your Watchlist
So, you found about 20 stocks that satisfy your screening criteria. The number of course is variable, sometimes you will find 50 ideas, and sometimes none. But let's go with 20 as this number represents a typical *yield* from your research. This will give you a sense of how much to expect from each step of the process.

Many casual investors will pick a few stocks from the list they like and start investing. Stop. You cannot make a portfolio out of these 20 stocks. Not yet.

At this time, you need to go through each of these 20 ideas and do some preliminary research. Pull up the company snapshot on your broker platform, and skim through the financials. You could also use free finance portals for this such as Google Finance, Yahoo Finance, etc., although be wary as you will find the free information can be error prone and incomplete and you may walk away with wrong conclusions.

Out of these 20 stocks, you may come up with 2-3 stocks that you want to research further. Add them to your watchlist.

This part is very important. Resist the temptation to research the stocks you just added to the watchlist for another 2 days. You want your thinking to reset before you come back to these stocks. You do not wish to make mistakes because at this time you will not be able to view these stocks from other angles.

Why is this important? Because it involves your capital. Every little bit of % gain or % loss has a disproportionate effect in your long-term wealth due to compounding. You want to give yourself as much advantage in the beginning as possible.

Step 3: Deep Research the Watchlist Stocks and Estimate the Intrinsic Values
Now we are in business. This is the grunt work and with commitment, you will get to enjoy it over time. This should not be thought of as pushing paper or doing boring accounting work. Instead reframe the process. Think of this as hunting for treasure. Sure, you will be frustrated for most of the time you are engaged in this

process – but once you hit the jackpot, believe me, it more than makes up for the drudgery.

For a value investor, the most exciting times are 1. Finding great stocks to invest in, and, 2. Eventually selling the stock to the market for large profits.

You are hunting for treasures. You want to find it before others do. Once you do, take your share and keep quiet about it. The rest of the party will eventually catch up to you, and when they do, a feeding frenzy will ensue. This may be the time for you to sell them your treasure for more than what it is worth.

Coming back to the deep research part, you will make friends with the company's investor relations website. You will be able to download the Quarterly and Annual reports from the website. In many cases you will also be able to order printed copies. I find print copy useful as I can flip through pages, underline and highlight relevant sections, and cross reference data. You can take these physical reports to a coffee shop or to the beach, turn off your phone, and just work on it without any electronic interference.

Your research in each of the stock should be carried out over multiple days.
Day 1: Just briefly skim through the financial reports and highlight any sections you find noteworthy. You may take notes in the margins
Day 2: Look at some other stock you are also researching at the same time. Let this one sit
Day 3: Review the reports again, this time in much more depth. Go through line by line. Keep a notebook or journal ready by your side where you can list your questions that will come up so you can find the answers. What concerns you? Does something not add up? Do you understand the management's strategy? Do you think they even have a strategy? How does the sector or the market look to you? This process should take you anywhere between 2 hours to 24 hours of just reading, asking questions, cross referencing, making notes, etc.

Let it sit for a week.

This one week of time has given you an opportunity to do some ancillary investigations. Your Reticular Activation System is working to help you notice news articles, discussions, talking heads, company products in the stores or someone's possession, branding value, etc. There is no particular method to this. You want your thinking to move freely and go in directions that are unplanned and unpredictable. Believe me, this one-week period is where you will think of things that will make or break your investment thesis.

One week later, come back and run the numbers. Estimate the intrinsic value, calculate your margin of safety and if everything makes sense, plan a purchase strategy.

Buy the Stock and Wait for The Market to Correct Its Mistake
You found a terrific stock that is undervalued, you understand the business, and you think there is a very viable catalyst soon that will unlock the value in the stock.

What now?

You know you are going to buy the stock. But do you know how much of the stock you should buy? Do you have an exit plan for a) when things do not go as expected, and b) when things go as expected and you need to book profits at some point?

Ideally you need the following 3 things:

1. A target price where the stock is considered fully valued, and you are ready to exit at any time beyond this point. You will want to continue and hold for as long as the stock appreciates, so you need a process here to maximize your profits
2. The position size in this stock that is right for your portfolio. There are many ways of doing this – You can optimize for profits based on your expected returns and confidence level, or you can optimize for the inherent risk in the stock to make sure you do not introduce more risk in the portfolio than is necessary. At Value Stock Guide, we optimize to balance the risk in the portfolio. This makes the portfolio less volatile without sacrificing too much in the expected profits. Of course, either of these two ways of position sizing is light years better than buying random amount of stock based on your gut feel (which is what you may be doing right now).
3. You need to eliminate most of the downside risk that comes from the market or from the possibility that you may have inadvertently picked up a value trap. Some of the ways you can do this is to set volatility-based stop loss orders (so they do not trigger in normal trading, but will trigger if there is a market

distress) and time-based stop loss orders so you do not continue in a stock for a long time without rewards – the opportunity cost of tying up your capital starts to exceed the potential reward in the future

This is a short summary of the buying process for a stock. There are other details not included in here. For example, less liquid and smaller stocks require a tactical strategy to acquire the position that you want. In a lot of cases, stop loss orders can be counterproductive and so you need to be able to identify these cases and handle them properly.

Profit Handsomely Once the Market Discovers the Stock

I have been value investing for over 2 decades now, and for bulk of this period, I sold the stock as soon as it reached my predetermined sale price. This sale price was calculated based on my estimate of the intrinsic value. This is in line with what most value investors will tell you – sell your stock once it becomes fairly valued.

Over time my philosophy has changed somewhat.

You will find that when the market discovers a value stock and it starts to appreciate, in almost all cases it will continue to appreciate way beyond its fair value. The market over does it, both on the way down, and on the way up.

We now try to stay in the stock for as long as it continues to rise. We accomplish this using trailing stop losses where possible. We have a field-tested process to find out the appropriate levels to use for the stops for any given stock.

The idea is to extract as much value out of a stock as possible. Whether this is done by exploiting the gap between the market price and the intrinsic value, or by capitalizing on the momentum on the way up, ultimately, we are capitalizing on the market inefficiency in both cases, which is the essence of value investing.

How to Maximize Your Chances of Finding Great Values?

If you want to catch a lot of succulent fish, you should go where the fish are plentiful.

You cannot find value where value does not exist. There may be rare situations that disprove my point, absolutely, but I would rather fish in the right waters then to belabor the point.

The vast swathes of the stock market have been beaten down to death. Large and mid-capitalization stocks are being followed by 100s of analysts of all different persuasion. They are being talked about on television and around the water coolers across the country. There are computer algorithms exploiting any valuation gap or opportunities at sub-second scale. I do not believe I have a faster trigger than a supercomputer connected to the exchange a foot away with optical cables that can perform trillions of what-if simulations per second. I do not wish to waste my time investing in the parts of the market where I do not have any advantage at all. I am actually worse off because I will pay for the privilege of receiving a slightly below market returns (index funds, etfs, most mutual funds).

Over 90% of the investors do precisely this. I do not wish to try and fix their behavior. Why should I? It is this mass hysteria that leads the herd to the same funds and investments, that makes it possible for value investors like us to profit handsomely.

The Profit Equation for value investors look like this:

Outstanding Profits = Buy good value stocks that are being ignored + Sell these stocks when they are no longer being ignored

This is Buy Low/Sell High in its purest form.

The key to finding good value stocks is to investigate the corners of the market that are being ignored. These tend to be small beaten down companies.

These companies have the following characteristics that make them so attractive to us:

1. They are not very well followed on the wall street
2. They are less liquid. This is a benefit. I will repeat, this is a benefit. You have more control over your buying and selling and can be patient and let the price come to you, if you know what you are doing. You are NOT at the mercy of algorithmic traders
3. The companies and the businesses are easy to understand. I know that if I end up buying the whole company accidentally, I will probably do a better job with it than the management today. I do not want to, but yes, this is helpful to know
4. There are so many of them. There are times when you may run out of ideas, but you will still have more ideas than if you were investing in large company stocks

5. In most cases, wall street actually creates undervaluation. It is quite predictable that a small division being spun off will be sold by the funds for no valuation-based reason and will be undervalued 3 months after the spinoff occurs.
6. These are less risky. More volatile maybe, but the risk of capital loss is smaller because your due diligence is better, and these stocks are less correlated with the market. They do not suddenly crash because someone tweets something at 3 am
7. You can pick up the phone and could potentially talk to the CFO or the CEO of the company and get your questions answered

There is now a new trend of "factor investing". This identifies different factors that lead an investor to beat the market over time. Some of the factors are "observed" and possibly transient – the advantage will disappear as more investors start chasing these factors. Other factors have stood the test of the time. The 2 factors that we target include 1) value and 2) size

Let's examine the historical evidence for focusing your investments in the small value asset class in the next chapter.

THE SECRET TO BEATING THE MARKET BY 6% OVER THE LONG TERM: BUY THE RIGHT ASSET CLASS

> Within the novel Life, the Universe and Everything of Douglas Adams' The Hitchhiker's Guide to the Galaxy science fiction series, his character Ford Prefect describes somebody else's problem as:
>
>> *An SEP is something we can't see, or don't see, or our brain doesn't let us see, because we think that it's somebody else's problem.... The brain just edits it out, it's like a blind spot. If you look at it directly you won't see it unless you know precisely what it is. Your only hope is to catch it by surprise out of the corner of your eye.*
>
> The narration then explains:
>
>> *The technology involved in making something properly invisible is so mind-bogglingly complex that 999,999,999 times out of a billion it's simpler just to take the thing away and do without it....... The "Somebody Else's Problem field" is much simpler, more effective, and "can be run for over a hundred years on a single torch battery."*
>>
>> *This is because it relies on people's natural predisposition not to see anything they don't want to, weren't expecting, or can't explain.*

Douglas Adams might as well be talking about the investments industry.

There are entire industries built upon the premise that investors cannot reliably beat the market. The success of these funds and ETFs depend on ignoring the research that inconveniently says otherwise, and they spend tremendous amount of media time reinforcing this premise on the retail investor. The premise of course is flawed but we have learned to not see this.

The Reality is That Given Sufficient Time, and Patience and Discipline, Any Investor can Beat the Market. Of course, there is a logical limit. Everyone cannot be above average. But the math is beautiful – the asset class that lets you outperform the market is precisely the asset class that institutions cannot invest significant amounts in – so if you are not "convinced" that mostly large cap funds and ETFs and stocks are the only way to invest, you have every chance to generate returns that put Wall Street to shame.

Warren Buffett, Benjamin Graham, Shelby Davis and others like them are not unexplainable anomalies in stock market. These are the investors who chose to use common sense instead of relying on the academic theories that do not work that well in practice.

Let's start by examining the evidence.

There is a body of research that shows that over a long investment horizon, small cap stocks have outperformed their large cap brethren. At the same time, value stocks outperform growth. In one study, Ibbotson Associates studied the annual performance of stocks classified by size (large, mid, small and micro) as well as by style (growth and value) between the periods 1969 and 2002[1]. They found that the small cap value and microcap value stocks far outperform all other asset classes. At the same time, small cap growth and microcap growth are the worst performing asset class.

	Geometric Mean (%)	Arithmetic Mean (%)	Standard Deviation (%)	Sharpe Ratio
All Growth	8.79	10.72	20.25	0.21
All Value	10.99	12.31	17.08	0.34
Large-Cap Growth	8.9	10.91	20.75	0.21
Large-Cap Value	10.43	11.75	17	0.31
Mid-Cap Growth	8.88	11.09	21.88	0.21
Mid-Cap Value	13.03	14.66	19.37	0.42
Small-Cap Growth	8.2	11.04	24.77	0.18
Small-Cap Value	14.35	16.41	21.69	0.46
Micro-Cap Growth	6.47	10.2	28.66	0.13
Micro-Cap Value	14.66	17.44	24.69	0.44

Another interesting insight from this table is that for every capitalization class, the value stocks have smaller standard deviation from the mean, which implies that value stocks carry less risk than their growth counterparts with similar sized companies.

Looking at the Sharpe Ratio, which measures risk adjusted returns, it is striking to see the difference between the highest performing asset class (Small-Cap Value)

---

[1] Ibbotson Style Indices: A Comprehensive Set of Growth and Value Data, 2003 (on the web)

and the lowest performing asset class (Micro-Cap Growth). ***Small Cap Value stocks have historically returned highest returns for any level of risk you are willing to take in your investments.***

Another study[2] that measured asset class performance between 1927 and 2005 confirms a similar pattern.

	Value	Growth
Large Cap	9.21%	6.17%
Small Cap	12.13%	5.77%
Total Stock Market	6.72%	

Still, investors continue to focus on finding the next explosive growth story. For every Microsoft or Cisco Systems, there are literally hundreds of growth stocks that fizzle out. Odds of finding that one stock that will secure your retirement is slim, perhaps even less than the odds most casinos give you.

Why do Small Cap Value Stocks Perform So Much Better?

If you follow the Efficient Market Hypotheses, you would assume that if the markets are efficient, then any source of out-performance will be quickly eliminated as investors discover these stocks and pile on. However, there are very practical reasons why this does not happen in the real world.

1. Small Cap Value stocks are generally very boring companies that no one has heard of. These are unglamorous companies, unlikely to garner much oohs and ahhs around the dinner table
2. Investors overreact to growth prospects and bid up the shares high. That is why growth stocks are expensive and provide smaller returns. On the flip side, investors overreact and force the smaller value stocks down at the slightest whiff of bad news or general discomfort.
3. There is insufficient coverage of these stocks on the Wall Street due to smaller size and lack of liquidity. As a result, they escape the attention of most institutional and retail investors who depend on brokers or sell side analyst's recommendations

---

[2] Why does small value do so well (on the web)

4. Most institutions and funds are not allowed to own small cap and micro-cap stocks and if they do come into possession of any such stock, perhaps due to a spin off, they are forced to sell off their position

Due to these reasons, there is little investor interest in small cap stocks. But enterprising value investors know that small caps offer the best places to find true value stocks that will on average comfortably beat the market over the long term.

The 2 Components of the Out Performance for Small Cap Value Stocks

The two long term trends from the performance data presented above is immediately visible.

1. Smaller the stock, greater the performance, and,
2. Value does better than growth

Size Premium has been said to exist that says that the small company stocks tend to outperform the large company stocks on a risk-adjusted basis. This premium seems to come and go, but a recent paper suggests that if you adjust for the quality of the companies, size premium does exist and can be significant.

Value Premium was ironically discovered by Fama and French, the postulators of the Efficient Market Hypothesis, as an anomaly that the Efficient Market Hypothesis cannot explain. Fama and French went on to win the Nobel Prize for their work on the Efficient Market Hypothesis that made the whole passive index fund investing industry grow explosively. If the markets are efficient, why bother with individual stock picking, right?

So, we have a choice.

We too can ignore 80+ year of history and the persistence of the size and value premiums as something that cannot be explained and go with the crowds and invest in the usual index funds or other pseudo index funds.

Or we can decide that the anomalies are the bits that are more interesting than the bits that are efficient. It is hard work to research these companies, as other investors are busy looking away, these stocks do not get enough research coverage. The rewards, thankfully, compensates handsomely for any effort we put in this area.

Finding Promising Small Cap Value Stocks

With the coverage of these stocks so scant, a value investor literally needs to comb through the entire universe of small cap stocks to find promising candidates. With each of these stocks, the investor needs to go through the public filings and annual reports to understand the company, analyze the business and its financials and figure out a reasonable valuation of the company. Once this research in small cap stocks is complete, it is a matter of purchasing those stocks that offer good value and patiently wait for the market to understand its folly and discover these stocks. This is time and labor-intensive work for most investors and a typical investor is not willing to patiently sit on his or her shares for a long time if immediate returns are not visible.

PRINCIPLE 2: RISK MANAGEMENT AND CORRECT POSITION SIZING IS ONE OF THE KEY DRIVERS OF PROFITS

Suppose you and a friend decide to invest in 2 stocks

Stock 1, XYZ doubles after a year from where both of you purchased it

Stock 2, ABC loses 50% of its value a year from where both of you purchased the stock

At the end of the year, you both compare notes. Your friend is happy with how his portfolio turned out. You, on the other hand, have lost quite a bit and you do not understand why there is so much difference in the outcome when both of you invested in the same stock and paid the same price.

Let's add some more detail and flesh this out a bit more to understand what is going on.

Your Portfolio: Starting Capital = $10,000, Ending Capital = $9,500, Return: -5%

Stock/Asset	Allocation	Invested Capital	Return	Final Value
ABC	20%	$2000	-50%	$1000
XYZ	5%	$500	100%	$1000
Cash	75%	$7500	0%	$7500

Your Friend's Portfolio: Starting Capital = $10,000, Ending Capital = $11,750, Return: +17.50%

Stock/Asset	Allocation	Invested Capital	Return	Final Value
ABC	5%	$500	-50%	$250
XYZ	20%	$2000	100%	$4000
Cash	75%	$7500	0%	$7500

You are happy for your friend's 17.5% gain over the year. You realize that this difference is significant, and it all came down to 1 simple thing. You chose different position sizes than your friend did.

I will let this sink in for a little bit.

Picking the right stock is important, obviously, but how much you invest in this stock vis-à-vis other stocks in your portfolio, is what will determine if you eventually end up making all your life dreams come true, or whether you give up investing in disgust, and find odd jobs in your retirement to pay your bills.

Just as your gains compound, your mistakes also compound. The market is relentless. If you keep repeating the same mistakes again and again, soon you will be left with nothing.

How Could You Have Avoided This?

There are two different ways you can address this.

1. Use Kelly Criterion: This is a mathematically guaranteed way of sizing your positions in such a way that you maximize your gains over a long period of time. This also avoids complete wipeouts. To use this well, you need be very good at estimating your probabilities of winning on any given investment and the size of the expected win. The estimation of probabilities and size of expected win will come once you have enough investments in your track record that you can analyze (Around 100 to start, more is better). Most value investors do not have this much data to go through. They want to rely on their gut feel for these values, but for this to work, you should have a lot of experience. If you work Kelly Criterion well, you will make a lot of money. It will make your portfolio very volatile and very concentrated, and you need the mental fortitude to be able to sleep at night. It is rumored that Warren Buffett uses Kelly Criterion
2. Use Volatility based Risk Parity method: In this method you decide how much you are willing to risk on any given stock. This value comes from a study of the stock's volatility. Then you place stops to ensure that you do not end up risking more than what you planned for. You are equalizing risk across your entire portfolio. For highly volatile stocks, you will end up purchasing less of them. For less volatile stocks, you will purchase more. Your rewards potential for each stock does not change and it is based on your estimate of the valuation gap

In the example above, you could have allocated more to the stock that was likely to do better. But probably you had no way of knowing this or even estimating this. In such a case, if you had exited the stock ABC once it lost, let's say, 10% of your investment, you would still have come out with a profit in your portfolio after one year.

As you see, the guidance above is very directional. I tell you what you should do and why, and I will provide some more guidance on numbers and values in the next chapter. However, you have your own unique situation and can tolerate less or more risk than I do. You will just have to start using these principles and over time you will be able to see what makes you uncomfortable, and then you tweak a parameter here, and a parameter there. This is a process that requires getting your feet wet in the market, make mistakes, take both risks and rewards as they come, and get better over time.

Soon enough, you will have an investment process that just works consistently, day in and day out, and that is perfectly matched to you.

HOW WE USE THE VOLATILITY BASED RISK PARITY METHOD AT VALUE STOCK GUIDE TO SIZE POSITIONS CORRECTLY AND MANAGE RISK?

This involves a little math so bear with me.

The volatility-based Risk-Parity method seeks to equalize the risk across the portfolio. The main goals are

1. Determine how much of the portfolio we are willing to lose in any given position
2. Determine the initial risk (based on volatility), in the stock that we are buying we will be willing to assume, and place a stop loss at this level,
3. As the stock price appreciates, we move the stop loss levels higher. Once we reach the full valuation (the price where we deem the stock to be overvalued and should be sold), we continue to trail the stock price with stop loss levels, but the stops are now placed at smaller distance from the current price

The key here is to determine the value of Initial Risk and everything falls in place.

Let me take you through an example:

R = ATR (average true range – the average price movement in the stock over the past 2 weeks)

Initial Risk = $S*N*R$, where N depends on your risk tolerance, and S is the number of shares you should purchase

Initial Risk is also = X% of your portfolio. You choose the value of X based on what you are comfortable with losing if this stock falls and is sold at the stop loss price.

If you are very risk averse, you might pick N = 2 or 3. Value investors will likely have N between 6 and 10.

If you are very risk averse, you will choose X% to be very small, 1% or below.

Example of Position Sizing: Using Some Real Numbers,

Let's say you have a $100,000 portfolio. And you have decided that you are willing to lose a maximum of 1% on any given stock.

Suppose you are considering MSFT stock. Its current price is $105.43. Its ATR is 1.6

You can pull up the 1-year chart of any stock on Yahoo Finance and plot the Average True Range. The following is the chart for MSFT as of July 13, 2018 taken from Yahoo Finance, with the ATR indicator added at the bottom (read the number at the end of the ATR line)

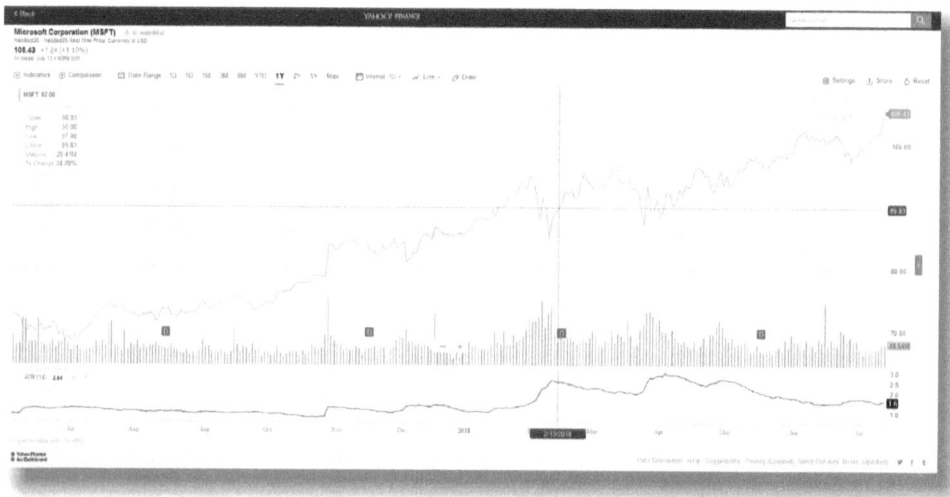

Let's also assume that you have chosen the value of N=10. This means that you will let the stock price fall 10 times the ATR before you will consider selling the stock with a Stop Loss order.

In this case,

Initial Risk = 1% of portfolio = $1000 = S*10*1.6,

Or S = $1000/(10*1.6) = 62 shares.

Therefore, you will invest 62 * $105.43= $6536.66 in MSFT stock, or roughly 6.5% of your portfolio.

For stocks that are more volatile, this method will force you to allocate a smaller part of your portfolio. For less volatile stocks, you allocate a larger part of your portfolio. This is how your risk across all your positions are equalized.

You will place your initial stop loss at 10*ATR or $16 below the current price. In this case, this is at $89.43

This ensures that you will never lose more than 1% of your portfolio in MSFT stock (or any other stock you own in your portfolio selected using this method)

Uh oh, Don't Value Investors Buy More When the Stock Gets Cheaper?
Absolutely!

We do not wish to be forced into a sale every time the stock price declines. In fact, we would like to buy more if the stock becomes more undervalued. This is a delicate dance – you must choose the value of N appropriately.

If you wish to protect from selling out of a stock unnecessarily, choose a larger value of N. Just remember that this means that you will be able to buy less number of shares of the stock, so that your overall portfolio risk remains under control.

If you are more risk tolerant than you thought, you may choose to risk more than 1% of your portfolio to one stock. 2%, 3%, etc. Choose your own number after you have had experience with this method and can truly assess what you are comfortable with.

Capturing the Maximum Upside
Value Investors are notorious for selling too early. A classic value investor might argue that once a stock reaches its fair price, there is no justification to hold on. I think it is not necessary to leave profits on the table and while we cannot consistently choose to exit at the top, we can certainly institute processes that regularly takes us as high as we can go.

How do we do this?

As the stock price appreciates, consider moving the Stop Loss level higher. You may wish to keep the Stop Loss distance at 10ATR, if this was your initial risk.

Once the stock price moves above your "fair value estimate", you can narrow your stop loss to 3ATR (for example), since at these levels you will be okay to sell if the price declines, but in case it appreciates further, you are now able to accrue additional profits.

With this method, your returns are at least as good as a regular value investor, but most likely significantly better.

What About Using the Kelly Criterion?

Kelly Criterion was developed by John Kelly at Bell Labs. It has been proven to maximize the portfolio growth over time compared to *any other strategy*.

It is rumored that Warren Buffett and Bill Gross use Kelly Criterion or some modified version of it.

This is how it works:

Assume,

- f is the fraction of the current capital you have available to invest
- b is the odds of winning (if you succeed, the value of your investment increases from 1 to $1 + b$)
- a is the odds of losing (value decreases from 1 to $1 - a$)
- p is the probability of winning, and,
- q is the probability of losing, or $1 - p$

Then, you should invest

$f = p/a - q/b$ of your portfolio in this stock.

Over time, this will theoretically give you the best growth in your portfolio possible.

There are several considerations if you want to use the Kelly Criterion

1. You need to have a long track record and well-established process to properly estimate the probability of winning. The probability of winning here is primarily a function of how your investments tend to perform over time. Do you make winning investments 75% of the time? Then p for you is 0.75
2. The portfolio using Kelly Criterion can be VERY concentrated and volatile. For example, if $p = 0.75$ and your odds of losing is 50% and odds of winning is 50% (very common, value is halved in the worst case or doubled in the best case), Kelly Criterion asks you to invest $0.75/0.5 - 0.25/0.5 = 1$ or your entire portfolio in this stock. This makes sense because 3 out of 4 times you will double your investment. In practice, this can be a nightmare for someone who is no able to tolerate this much volatility

3. While mathematically, using Kelly Criterion means your portfolio will never go to zero, the volatility will be unnerving
4. Investors who do use Kelly Criterion tend to use ½ - Kelly. This means using half of the fraction the Kelly Criterion recommends. This is not as good as full Kelly, but it makes the portfolio more stable without sacrificing too much in the long-term returns.

At Value Stock Guide, we evaluated these 2 methods and chose to use the Volatility based Risk Parity Method for portfolio sizing and risk control. Premium members participate in this portfolio sizing and risk control process.

Pop Quiz: Ever wonder why investors who follow Warren Buffett's stock picks do not come close to performing as well as Buffett does?

Answer: Because they do not have the position sizing and risk management process that Buffett uses.

If you decide to use a service to recommend stocks to you, and you do not come close to replicating their returns, it is very likely that your position sizing is very different from what the service uses. How would you know what position size to use? Make sure your service gives you this information, like we do at Value Stock Guide.

PRINCIPLE 3: EVERY LITTLE BIT MATTERS. WE TAKE ALL MEASURES NECESSARY TO IMPROVE THE ODDS OF PROFIT AND ELIMINATE AS MUCH RISK IN THE PORTFOLIO THAT WE CAN

Compounding is a beautiful thing when it is working for you. When it works against you, the results are equally devastating.

Most of us muddle through our investments because we do not have any coherent strategy. We may pick a few good stocks and enjoy some nice returns. But we may not have maximized our potential. On the other hand, we may end up losing enough on a single stock that undoes all the hard work we put into our portfolio that year.

In short, there is no strategy.

Hopefully the first 2 chapters get you started on building a solid workable strategy. You do not need to be perfect when you start. Just having a well-defined strategy will put you on the correct profitable path.

Over time you will find that small decisions here and there have disproportionate influence on your returns.

Consider the following two scenarios:

Scenario 1: You start with $100 and increase its value by 1% every day by following good investment practices, and,

Scenario 2: You start with $100 and destroy 1% of the value every day by simple errors in judgement

Frankly, at the end of the week, you wouldn't see the point of what I am saying. The difference between these 2 scenarios is quite small. Easily manageable you would think.

After 7 days of this, Scenario 1 has your $100 grow to $107.21.
After 7 days of this, Scenario 2 has your $100 become $93.21

At this time, you may think, "okay fine. But this is not the end of the world. In fact, just 1 good day in the market for Scenario 2 can totally change the picture"

Sure, it can. I do not doubt that. However, you are now giving up your control to the market.

Just remember, compounding is relentless. If you do not change your processes and fix your errors of judgement, at the end of a year (Day 365),

Scenario 1 will grow your portfolio to $3778.34
Scenario 2 will shrink your portfolio to $2.55

Sound far-fetched?

It is quite possible. There are countless examples of investors and traders who have gone ahead and destroyed their entire capital in a short order. In many cases, it does not even take 1 year for them to do this. Perhaps you know some of them in your own peer group.

So, what is my point?

Very simply, once you have decided on the strategy, stick with the strategy.

For example, if your strategy says you should sell the stock at a certain price, if the stock reaches this price, sell.

Do not waffle. Do not think that the conditions are now different. You set that order for a reason, follow through with it.

Later if you determine that your strategy needs to be amended, sure, do that. You are now deciding when you are in control and you are doing this because you have reason and data that indicates a change needs to be made. You are not being reactive.

I will even assert that if you follow the proper position sizing and risk management techniques, you can do reasonably well even if you randomly pick your stocks. Value investing will help you take your returns to the next level, but a random picking process will also work and keep you profitable, *if you develop good investment habits and apply them consistently. They are so important!*

If you are not sure what these good investing habits are, please find some one that has been successful, so you can learn from this person. I have listed quite a few in this document (proper due diligence with an objective eye, focus on rewards, choose your position sizes properly, manage your risks, etc). You can read more on ValueStockGuide.com website, or just email me when you have questions and I will do my best to answer them quickly.

> The *VSG Premium service* I offer takes you through this process and gives you actual stocks you should invest in. I calculate the correct position sizes for you and give you all the information you need to set up your risk management processes. It is truly done for you. All you must do is to follow the advice you receive from me in your email. If you wish to get more involved, you can log in to your account on the Value Stock Guide website and access the full research report for each stock. You can also participate in a forum exclusive to Premium members and discuss the portfolio stocks, ask questions, etc.
>
> How would you like to have a very high performing stock portfolio, that maximizes rewards and minimizes risk, and has a track record that has bested all major market indices and Berkshire Hathaway since inception?
>
> If this is something you are interested in, please *visit the membership information page*. Please note that while anyone can sign up for the Perspectives service, I am very selective about the number of people and who I accept in the Premium program.

In Conclusion

You should take away two main learnings from this eBook so far.

Great investment results are almost guaranteed to those who

1. Maximize their chances of finding great profitable value stocks, and,
2. Structure their portfolio to maximize returns and minimize risk, and,
3. Adopt good investing habits and stick to them consistently

While you will not be able to remove all barriers to investment success, there are tools and techniques you can use to get you close and it will change your investment results for better drastically.

Next, we will look at some of the myths that you as an investor are constantly subjected to in the media, at your financial adviser's office, and elsewhere. You will see that these myths work to keep you poor while enriching the investments industry.

MYTH #1: STOCK MARKETS ARE EFFICIENT

That blip you see over there? In an efficient market, this should not happen

Investors are constantly reminded that the markets are efficient and there is no use trying to beat the market as it cannot be done on a consistent basis. In fact, we are told, that over 70% of the mutual funds fail to beat the market, presenting this as an evidence to somehow imply, in some convoluted logic, that we are better off handing over our money to the same mutual funds and invest passively, rather than take control of our own portfolio. I find this argument even more vacuous, considering that the best investors and stock pickers, who also happen to manage significant sums of money, do not usually run mutual funds.

But Is the Market Truly Efficient?

The Efficient Market Hypothesis states that the securities prices reflect all publicly available information. Trading based on insider knowledge is illegal, and even if it were possible, not enough investors would be privy to such nonpublic information to make any significant impact on the overall returns of any stock. If Efficient Market Hypothesis were true, wouldn't it imply that no investor has any advantage over any other when it comes to investing in stocks? If security prices immediately adjust to reflect any new public information than perhaps the only predictor to stock performance is the amount of risk an investor is willing to take.

Indeed, most financial products available to the investors today tacitly assume the sanctity of the Efficient Market Hypothesis. Passive investing, diversification and overall market index as a benchmark for performance are all a result of a blind faith in the EMH. Or to put it another way, if what you know about the past of the company doesn't matter (since the stock price already reflects it), and there is no way of reliably knowing the future of the company, you might as well invest in a basket of stocks to cancel out individual stock risk and let your portfolio ride on the market risk alone.

No wonder index funds and passive investing are such easy sells. The financial industry has all the incentive to continue to promote the EMH and use it as an excuse for their own incompetence.

History Paints a Different Picture

Many studies on historical performance of stocks classified by asset classes have shown that over a reasonably long periods of time small cap stocks tend to outperform large cap stocks and value stocks outperform growth stocks. Traditionally, this has been brushed aside by asserting that small cap stocks and value stocks are riskier than the market, so it is not surprising that the returns are higher. However, a study by Ibbotson Associates (now part of Morningstar) goes even further and shows that small cap value stocks outperform all other asset classes on **risk-adjusted basis**.

Professor Greenwald in his seminal book *Value Investing: From Graham to Buffett and Beyond (Wiley Finance)* shows that if investors had blindly bought a portfolio of the lowest Price to Book ratio stocks they would have done better than the market. Even a slight introduction of a value bias improves portfolio performance.

So, if the Markets are Efficient, how can this be?

Markets are efficient in aggregate and they are also reasonably efficient for well understood companies with highly liquid stock. For a large company that has a good number of Wall Street analysts following it, it is understandable that almost everything that is known is reflected in the stock price. Liquidity in the stock ensures that complex computer-generated trades continuously work to exploit any inefficiency that may occur from time to time and quickly erase it.

However, there are quite a few situations where the markets are not as efficient, and one can find stocks that are truly undervalued if one is alert. Here are a few cases where this is true

- **Small cap stocks that are not well followed** – Large institutions such as mutual funds and pension funds tend to avoid these stocks. Typically, these funds avoid buying meaningful stakes in any company as that comes with additional filing requirements and the responsibilities of being a large shareholder. A smaller stake may not make sense for a large fund as any performance advantage of these stocks will just be a blip on their overall portfolio. They are also not covered adequately by the Wall Street as some of these companies are too small to be a investment banking prospect.
- **Industry, sector or stock specific bull or bear market** – In short term, the market overdoes its exuberance or pessimism for certain sectors or even individual companies. Eventually, the market does settle at the correct valuation, but the discrepancy may persist for a long time. For example, the real estate bubble lasted much longer than expected. Even after it was plainly clear to most market observers that a bubble exists, most institutions could not simply unwind their positions quickly as that would cause an immediate market collapse. A retail investor can move much more quickly than an institution in these situations and take advantage of the gap between price and value.
Certain cyclical industries go through a boom to bust cycle regularly. Metals, commodities, shipping, etc. are a few examples. If an investor can determine that the demand of the product is not eroding, but rather the sector is doing badly due to excess capacity and over supply issues, than it is just a matter of waiting out until the capacity/supply imbalances are corrected for the stocks to recover. If you do your research right, these can be potentially phenomenal stocks to buy and wait for the cycle to repeat.
- **Unwanted stocks, special situation stocks** – A stock is sold off by funds when they no longer fit the charter of the fund. This is generally done regardless of the investment merit of the stock. When this happens, a small window of undervaluation is created, that can reward investors handsomely. The following are some of the few common situations where this happens:
    - A stock leaves a popular index causing all the funds that invest in this index to sell the stock
    - A large company spins off a small division and the funds holding the parent company are not interested in the smaller spun off company
    - Mergers and acquisitions involving part or all the acquired company where the market is not clear about the fundamentals of the business being acquired
- **Aggressively marketed stocks** – If there is one example of a situation where sellers are privy to more information about the company than the buyers are, it is the IPO market. This is one case where insider selling is

legal, and it is not a surprise that the buyers in the IPO markets generally lose. Perhaps if a sector is witnessing a lot of IPO activity, an investor might take it as a sign of an overheated market and sell any holdings in that sector (or avoid it like a plague).

Market inefficiencies create undervaluation that an investor can buy into. In some other cases, it can also create overvaluation that an investor can sell into or avoid. It is beneficial for a self-managed investor to be alert for these situations as the difference in performance between a value biased portfolio and a market neutral portfolio can be very significant over the life of the portfolio. Make sure you look for investments outside of the typical Wall Street research and research the company deeply to understand its business and prospects. If the stock has been left for dead, but the business is humming along, it can be a terrific investment. These are the hidden corners of the market where the best stock picks lie and if you do not look for them yourself, you will never find them

And this is why Warren Buffett and other investors believe that the small investors have great advantage over the Wall Street. We are largely unconcerned with such things as stock liquidity, float, market caps, etc. which often stymie the large institutions. We can focus solely on the business fundamentals for our investment decisions.

MYTH #2: MERE MORTALS LIKE YOU AND I CANNOT BEAT THE MARKET

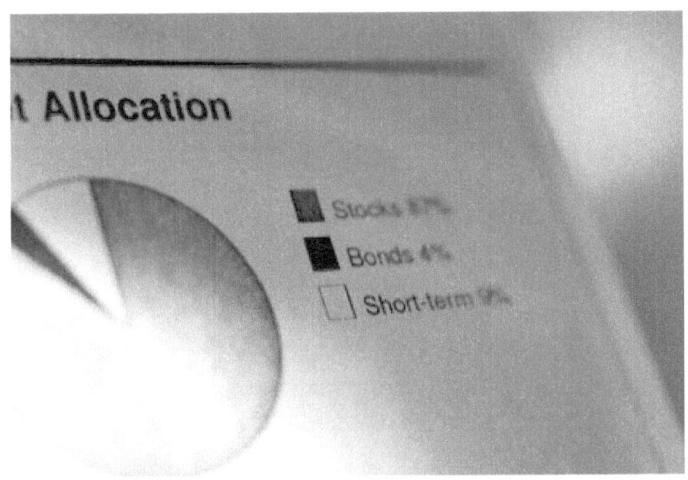

Pies that feed your financial advisor

Most of the mutual fund industry and the financial planning establishment will have you believe that the only smart way to invest is passive investing, that is, buy into a heavily diversified portfolio and rebalance your portfolio periodically to achieve the perfect asset allocation. This assertion is often backed up by statistics and research that seem to offer support for the two most widely promoted apparent truisms in investing:

1. Achieving average market returns is acceptable and a worthwhile goal, and
2. To get higher returns, you must take on higher risk

Consider also the Efficient Market Hypothesis that essentially implies that there are no stock picking strategies that provide a sustainable advantage for an investor over any long period of time. The markets will immediately react to close any "inefficiency" in the market. You would therefore think that your best bet for investing success is to buy into an index fund and hope for the best.

Let's take a brief look at both these points.

Passive Investing Claim #1: Achieving Average Market Returns is Acceptable and a Worthwhile Goal

So many *experts* agree that you should aspire to be average and anything else is foolish and a pipe dream. So what statistics they use to back up this claim?

80% of the Mutual Funds run by Professional Investors Fail to Beat the Market

80% number is stunning but if you stop to think about it for more than a minute, it is hardly surprising.

Consider the following:

- The best and the smartest investors prefer to run hedge funds and not mutual funds. Sure, there are some great mutual fund managers but they more likely than not are already part of the 20% that beat the market
- Great mutual funds tend to attract more investor dollars and are therefore also much larger than your average loser funds. The 20% of the funds that beat the market typically manage more than 20% of the total invested monies in their funds
- Mutual funds ARE one of the largest components of the stock market and it is not surprising that their average returns will approximate the average market returns
- With so much capital invested in index funds (which will fail to beat the market just because of the fees) it is even more difficult for average mutual fund returns to better the market

Now think of the fund managers who do have a history of generating market beating returns. This would include Peter Lynch, Ken Heebner, Marty Whitman, Bill Miller, etc. There is something they all have in common – they are or were all excellent stock pickers who usually ran a concentrated portfolio to generate market beating returns. Perhaps Peter Lynch is an exception to the concentrated portfolio requirement, but it is to his credit that he continued to deliver excellent returns long after the Magellan Fund started growing too large and this is largely since he was an above average stock picker.

Diversification is necessary if you don't know which stocks to pick, don't have time to research investments, or, as is the case of the most fund managers, you fear underperforming your index and your job or compensation depends on it.

Now think of a typical financial planner or your friendly neighborhood broker. It is just so easy for them to follow the herd and the conventional wisdom than to risk losing a client by giving a different advice which might be considered "risky".

But there is a much more fundamental question, you as an investor need to ask yourself. Your wealth, retirement and future lifestyle depend on your investments. *Why would you accept average or mediocre in this area of your life when you will not accept average or mediocre in any other part of your life?*

You say risk? Let's talk about risk for a moment (a great segue to discussing the next point).

Passive Investing Claim #2: To Achieve Higher Returns, You Have to Take on Higher Risk

This is so often stated as a fact that it really boggles my mind to think that people really believe this. It is like saying "You can't get better grades at school unless you take more risk" or "Only way to make a business more successful is to take more risk"! There is no credit given to the fact that ability, hard work, and smarts can remove a lot of risk from any endeavor. Buying stocks is not the same as buying a lottery ticket where taking more risk (that is buying more tickets or numbers) increases your chance of a substantial payout. Stocks do not perform randomly.

To understand what is going on here, we will need to understand how risk is defined in investing.

Risk is traditionally associated with beta or the volatility of the stock price on a daily basis as compared to the market index. Any stock that closely tracks the market is considered average risk while a stock with prices less volatile with that of the market index is considered less risky and vice versa. For a casual investor, it does reinforce the notion that being as risky as the market is normal and acceptable, but this is not even the worst of the problem with this definition of risk. Consider the stock whose price has been beaten down to a very low point. Just like Washington Post was when Buffett bought a stake in the company. The entire company could be bought at a mere $100 million at that time. This definition of risk would have you believe that Washington Post was riskier at $100 million market capitalization than it was some time earlier at a higher market value.

To me, the risk that a stock will perform much better than the market is a good risk that I want to take – not avoid.

Risk can be Mitigated with Due Diligence and Good Selection Process

If you treat stock prices as random and inherently unpredictable, then only way to lessen the risk in your portfolio is to diversify. But if you believe that stock prices ultimately reflect the strength of the underlying business, then a careful review of the business fundamentals will reveal how much real downside risk is really there if you choose to invest in the stock. Traditional value investors add another layer of conservatism by requiring a margin of safety – which just a way of saying that they will only pay a price that is much lower (30%-40% lower) than what they calculate as the intrinsic value of the stock.

Ultimately, the returns or the rewards depend on the effort and knowledge you bring to your stock picks. This is the same principle that applies to any other aspect of business or life.

References

- Professor Sharpe's argument in support of passive investing. Note the comparisons are with the returns of an average indexer versus an average active investor
- In support of active investing. Presents many arguments, in addition of rebutting Prof. Sharpe's paper referenced above
- A paper concluding average ETF investors underperform the index they are tracking. You can download the paper by clicking on the Download this Paper link on this page

The key takeaway from these referenced materials is that while passive investing sounds great on paper, in practice, active stock picking by careful long term-oriented investors wins out.

MYTH #3: EXCESSIVE DIVERSIFICATION IMPROVES RETURNS AND REDUCES RISK

Watch that basket carefully ...

Diversified Investments: When More is Less

Asset diversification, as it is practiced today, is a crutch.

From financial advisors, mutual fund industry, media, personal finance bloggers, and everyone in between, there is a consensus that diversification is essential for a good portfolio. Nothing can be further than the truth.

If You are Risk Averse, You Should Not be Investing in Stocks – Period

Investing in stocks is the same as investing in businesses on the expectation that the business will create value for the shareholders. Businesses create value by *taking risks*. This is the whole essence of a market economy – the rewards come in proportion to the amount of risk that is taken. Good businesses take intelligent risks, and those that do not go out of business eventually.

Good businesses also are keenly aware of the market dynamics, adjust their practices accordingly, and take on projects that minimizes overall risk profile of the business at any given time as much as possible. They also pursue new product lines and markets in search for value creation and risk reduction.

Investors in the stock market need to understand that if a business does not take risk to grow shareholder wealth, it is not worth investing in. There are no such thing as steady guaranteed returns with no risk. If that is what you want, you are better off in short term or high-quality bonds and money market instruments.

Diversification Does Not Even Address All Risk

Diversification, if done well, reduces the correlation between different assets so the volatility of the overall portfolio is moderated. Which means that if one stock in the portfolio drops significantly, the other non-correlated stocks that do not drop as much or increase in value will help the total portfolio avoid the extreme in the decline. Of course, it also works on the flip side – if a stock gains appreciably, the overall portfolio will not gain as much due to other stocks in the portfolio that have not performed as well. Diversification reduces portfolio volatility, so you can sleep better at night.

It does not increase your returns, but it just might decrease it. If you are a believer in diversified investments, and invest in say 100 different stocks, you have probably not done the amount of research and due diligence you should have done before investing in these stocks. It is also not possible for you to effectively monitor each stock in your portfolio. Add in your transaction fees and you have just traded some volatility in return for a portfolio that does not perform as well as it can.

And worse of all, no amount of diversification will save your portfolio from the "market risk". If the entire economy goes downhill, your portfolio will as well.

Boon for the Mutual Fund Industry

There are some mutual funds that rely on the good old stock picking skills to build a focused portfolio of names that they have a great deal of conviction in. The rest of the industry, and this being the majority, relies on diversification *to avoid losing to the index badly*. Some years they do better and some years they do worse. Overall though, there is not much to differentiate one mutual fund from another, except for the fees and expenses.

Most investors fear losing money more than they fear not making money. The concept of diversification speaks to these fears by promising less risk. And of course, mutual funds are great for diversification as they pool money and reduce costs of building a diversified portfolio. Lack of performance is explained away as an overall economic condition that the managers have no control over.

Put it another way, most investors are paying mutual fund managers for the privilege of running a ship that they can't control.

The situation is similar with financial advisors and the media. No one wants to invest time and research to build a great performing long-term portfolio if it means sometimes the portfolio might underperform the market significantly. So, everyone settles for the mediocre.

Buying Value Reduces Risk and Improves Performance

It is well documented that value investing outperforms growth, and small cap stocks outperform larger company stocks. In fact, small cap value stocks deliver better risk adjusted returns than all other asset classes. When you narrow down your investment selection by applying small cap and value filters, the selection is understandably going to be smaller. A 10 – 20 stock portfolio delivers adequate diversification if the stocks are chosen from diverse sectors. This helps moderate the portfolio volatility. Focusing on value and demanding a sufficient margin of safety reduces risk and increases performance over long term.

This also keeps your portfolio manageable, so you can properly research and monitor the businesses you own. It does mean more research and analysis to construct a focused portfolio but the rewards of spending some time upfront in due diligence and stock selection can be considerable

Bottom line

Diversify to reduce correlation between the stocks and the industries you are exposed to. 10 -20 stocks are sufficient for this. Anything higher and you enter into the territory of over-diversification which will reduce your returns as you cannot feasibly track all your stocks at this point. If you buy an index fund, remember that if you were going through each stock individually, you would not buy MOST of the stocks that the index fund holds because no investment thesis can be made for these stocks.

MYTH #4: COMPANY STOCK BUYBACKS ARE GOOD

Stock Buy backs can Destroy Value

If you are a shareholder, you generally welcome any share repurchase announcement. The math is simple, you think.

If the company remains valued at the same level in the market, the less number of shares this value is divided by, the more the value of the remaining shares. It is a way of engineering a higher share price.

What most investors forget to consider is that ***the company is using its own cash up to buy these shares back.***

These shares do not magically disappear.

So, while the numbers of shares do decline, the intrinsic value of the company also declines.

And not to mention any returns that the company could have generated if it had used that cash in alternative projects.

Why do Companies Buy Back Stock if they are Not Always the Best Use of Cash?

A shareholder should demand that the company they have entrusted their capital to uses it wisely. This means investing each dollar in projects that maximize the return on the capital.

When a company decides to buy back their own stock, they are indicating that the valuation is so distressed that investing in own shares are likely to generate better returns for the company (and the shareholders), then pursuing any other projects in their normal course of business. The problem is, that the company and the management often have an inflated sense of their worth.

They better be certain that the stock is undervalued by the market.

And they also need to be certain that there are no other better opportunities to use their cash.

There is no point paying $1.50 or $2 for an asset that is worth just a dollar.

You are better off parking the excess cash in treasuries and your shareholders will be richer for it.

You may well ask if a company has excess cash that it doesn't need, why they should not return it to the shareholders?

Fair question. Unless the stock is distressed, share repurchases are not the best way to return cash to the shareholders.

Just pay dividends, regular or a special onetime dividend.

It is a fair 1-1 exchange. Every $ in dividend payment transfers the same $ in value to the shareholders.

Income Taxes Should have Nothing to Do with Buyback vs Dividends Decision

The argument about the income tax treatment of the return of capital is something the company should not concern itself about. If that is the argument here, the tax impact is still much lower than the value destruction in buying back an overvalued stock (assuming a 10% incremental tax impact on capital gains vs dividend taxes, the over valuation in this case is comfortably more than 10%). The fact is, most investors have their own tax plans, and quite a few own shares in their tax deferred plans where the tax argument has no merit.

A Lot of Companies Make this Mistake

The fact is, top management of a company is not impartial. They always overestimate the prospects of their company and generally tend to believe that their stock is undervalued, *at any price*. Worse, a company maybe under a mistaken belief that their mandate is to support the stock price and not growing shareholder value

It all boils down to whether the management is short term focused or is looking after shareholder's interest for the long term.

Bottom-line: Look at Share Repurchases with a Critical Eye

Share repurchases can create value or they can destroy value. They are a great leveler and act as a catalyst to propel the stock price to the true value in the market.

If the stock is currently undervalued, it means it will see an appreciation. If the stock is currently overvalued, it will eventually decline as the value destruction becomes clear after the ill-advised stock buyback.

In any case, they also indicate if the management is fully grounded or if they have lost touch with reality.

MYTH #5: WE SHOULD AVOID STOCKS THAT ARE NOT VERY LIQUID

Small cap stocks generally have a liquidity problem.

This is one of the reasons why most investors stay away from small cap stocks. This is also one of the reasons why good undervalued stocks are easier to find in this asset class.

The market for highly liquid stocks is also normally highly efficient. The price you pay for the convenience of having your transaction execute in seconds (instead of hours or sometimes days) is returns that are at best average.

In my 18 years of investing in small cap value, I have found that lack of liquidity is hardly ever an issue. Part of it is just practicing good investing habits. The other part is understanding precisely what we are doing when investing in small cap value.

How to deal with lack of liquidity when buying the stock?

When you buy a small cap stock which is undervalued, you will find yourself in one of the following 2 situations.

1. **The price is low, and the selling is not yet done ("Blood in the streets")** – One of the recurring themes for most value investors is that they are often early into the buy. A stock may be undervalued now because of many factors (missed expectations, a lawsuit, declining market, etc.). If the price has fallen rapidly in the recent days, it means that there are more sellers than buyers at each price levels and the stock has not yet reached its equilibrium. If you determine that it is a good price to buy the stock at, *you are buying a stock that the market can't wait to get rid of*. You will not have any trouble at all executing your buy.
2. **The price is low, the volume is miniscule ("Nobody cares")** – Liquidity often dries up when all the sellers have sold. At a certain point, there may be interested buyers but very few sellers. Investors who currently own the stock have either bought lower recently or are not interested in selling because they share your investment thesis. Often, the stock just drifts along and there is not much interest in the market for this stock. If you are confident in your valuation thesis, this is the best time to buy the stock.

In either case, when you decide to buy, fix the price you want to pay and then set a limit order and keep it open until the order fills. In the first case, the limit order protects you from wild swings. In the second case, you set the limit order (GTC) as it might take a long time for the market maker to accumulate enough stock at your price to make a trade. Please note that other interested buyers are doing the same thing, but time is certainly on your side and patience is your greatest virtue.

How to deal with lack of liquidity when selling the stock?

Once you have purchased the stock for value, there are only two possible reasons why you would sell.

1. **Price has risen to reflect the value and you are harvesting your gains** – In majority of the cases when this happens, you will find that the liquidity of the stock has greatly improved. This being a small cap stock, it has now been discovered, articles are being written about the stock and the investors are rushing in. Perhaps an analyst or two have started coverage as well. Selling is not a problem at all since *you are selling the stock that the market can't wait to take off your hands*.
2. **You have found better uses for your money** – Perhaps a better stock, or you may have determined due to some reason that cash is a better investment than this stock. If the liquidity is still low, you will just have to execute your sell order patiently over time, like when you purchased the stock.

If you exercise requisite diligence in making an investment thesis, you will find that lack of liquidity, while real, is hardly ever a problem, *since most of the time you are doing the opposite of what the market is doing. On the contrary, with patience, you can get a better bargain then you can for a highly liquid stock.*

ADVICE #1: DO NOT USE BETA OF A STOCK AS PART OF YOUR INVESTMENT DECISIONS

For most investors who have grown up on the diet of high stock beta = high risk, this statement will come as a surprise. ***Beta means nothing for a stock***. And beta explains nothing about the investment merits of a stock.

Let me start with two thought experiments to drive this point home.

Scenario 1: Let's say you are interested in a stock that has declined significantly in the recent months. So much so that at this time, after you have done your research and due diligence, you conclude that the stock presents a compelling value. In fact, you conclude, that this investment is as sure a bet as any one is ever likely to get. The market has over done its selling, as it generally does when there is a investor panic.

Let's also spice it up a little and inject some specifics. This company, even though its stock has taken a beating, continues to generate more in free cash flow per year, than its entire market value, even after servicing its debt. You look deeper and find that after you clear away all the accounting clutter and GAAP mandated non-sense, the stock is priced at about 1 times net earnings per share.

In short, this is a bargain unlike any other.

Heck, if this level of undervaluation continues, the company can just decide to buy itself out and go private. That would be a very wise decision on their part. Alternatively, it is a very good acquisition for a smart corporate buyer. There is no way this kind of undervaluation will be allowed to continue. Sanity eventually returns.

Now the question is, if you decide to invest in this stock, are you taking enormous amounts of risk? The market thinks you are. The recent falling over the cliff of the stock price has pushed the stock's beta to beyond the threshold a rational investor would contemplate investing at. When the price starts moving up, it is likely going to be very volatile as well.

But you know that the risk here is close to zero. Just like Buffett thought the risk of investing in Washington Post was close to zero.

What do you think?

Scenario 2: Let's say you found a stock that no one cares about. It is a small company in the middle of nowhere in a boring industry. There is no analyst coverage, they have never been part of the Inc 500 and CEO owns so much of the company stock that it is almost like his family business. Which it was at one time.

In a quaint departure from the norm, the company management makes decisions that are decidedly long term. Some of these decisions involve capital expenses that will kill their next quarter's earnings, were it not for the fact that they do not worry about issuing guidance and there is no analyst breathing down their necks.

The company's balance sheet is like Fort Knox. Their margins lead the industry. It is a real gem. And the dividend is to die for. The management takes care of its shareholders.

You realize that the stock price today is much below where it ought to be given the company fundamentals. It is a great buy. And when some of the past capital investments start paying off, the company and the stock will be noticed. For the past few years, though, the stock has stayed sleepy and its beta is less than half of the market.

So, you buy the stock.

You know your risk is low, and the beta is low, so it all matches up. Right? But that is not why you bought the stock. You bought this stock because you expect the stock to provide a return that is significantly better than the market. And as the stock gets discovered, this return will come to you in fits and starts. The price may become volatile, but you know in the long run you will make handsome profits.

You bought the stock because you know you are buying it at a low and your downside is protected, but you want the beta to be high on the upside and you want to capture that upside.

Just to rile up the Efficient Market Hypothesis proponents a little more, I will lay out the 2 key rules of investing. Especially value investing.

1. Price $\neq$ Value, and
2. Volatility (beta) $\neq$ Risk

Besides, stock prices over the short term are essentially random and over long term are dictated by the fundamentals and the company performance in the future. The beta measures the past volatility of the stock and has no bearing on what the stock does in the future. A stock is not born with a beta assigned to it. Every stock moves through periods of high beta and low beta. The trick is to focus on the business fundamentals and find great opportunities to invest.

Where Does Beta Make Sense?

Beta makes sense in the context of a portfolio. You want to have enough diversity in your stock picks that your overall portfolio becomes less volatile by reducing correlation between your holdings. One way to do this is to get exposure to different industries that are not tied to each other. However, unless you are buying a mutual fund, you will still actively manage your investments based on their own individual investment merit. And if you are a value investor, you have already taken pains to not over pay and have therefore cut down a good chunk of your downside risk on each stock that you buy.

The volatility-based risk parity position sizing method we laid out earlier helps control the portfolio volatility. However, as you may have noticed, the volatility is not a factor when picking an individual stock. It only becomes a consideration once the stock is picked and needs to be integrated in the portfolio.

As Warren Buffett points out, cash and other "currency" investments are some of the lowest beta investments available, and they are the riskiest ones for preserving or enhancing your future purchasing power. What is more important is to judge the risk of capital loss before making any investment.

This chapter is quoted and referenced in the book **Mezzanine Financing: Tools, Applications and Total Performance** *by Professor Luc Nijs and published by Wiley Finance. Look for it in Chapter 3 which deals with the* **Intrinsic Cost of the Mezzanine Finance Products***.*

ADVICE #2: INVESTING RISK IS NOT WHAT YOU THINK IT IS

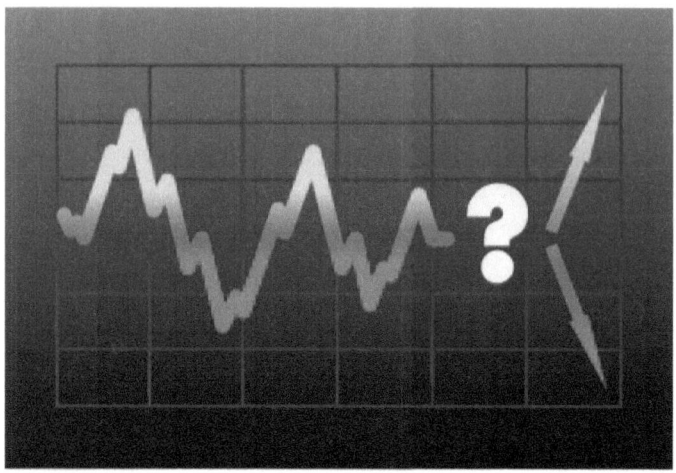

Investment risk rarely matches the risk perception in a security. Let's see why.

Held long enough, the price of a security approximates its value.

- Buying **overvalued stocks** in most cases deliver lackluster performance as the value struggles to catch up with the price. The price may decline, or if the business is growing value at a rapid pace, than perhaps there may be some price appreciation. Regardless, there is a better way to invest with less risk and more rewards
- Buying **undervalued stocks**, in most cases deliver outstanding performance over time as the price rises to catch up with the value – if the business continues to create value over time

The critical phrase here is "held long enough". We will discuss "risk" with this as a backdrop. For investors who are essentially short-term investors, looking for a quick profit, the value in the business does not matter much. When investing is not based on the underlying business fundamentals, it quickly becomes speculation. And speculation is notoriously hard way to create long term wealth on any sustained basis.

So, what is Risk?

Quite simply, risk is the possibility that the investment does not work out well. In some cases, you might have to wait longer than expected for the value to be realized. In other cases, you may even experience a loss of capital. Investment risk is essentially the downside risk of the security over your holding period.

This can happen for a number of reasons:

- **You make a mistake in building the investment thesis for the stock** – Value investing is more art than science. Mistakes can happen. You might over estimate the value of an asset, or under estimate the level of distress on the business. Or you just might have a misplaced decimal point in your spreadsheet. While it is essential to be as thorough as possible during the due diligence period, and lean on the conservative side, it is fool hardy to believe that the possibility of a mistake does not exist.
- **The market continues to stay irrational on the security** – Ever buy a stock that you think is a terrific value, and two years later, the stock is still a terrific value? I have. Although the stock has returned a quite respectable gain in these 2 years, the undervaluation persists. Some of the other stocks may be even less fortunate and the price might barely budge for years, even as the company fundamentals continue to improve.
- **Future may turn out to be different when you reach there** – Value investors try to protect against the uncertain future by paying more attention to the assets and asset quality and less credence to the earnings projections. There are still other ways your investment thesis may trip up. Economic conditions may change. Competition may intensify. FDA approvals may be withheld. Management may turn out to be corrupt.

How do you Protect Against these Risks?

The simplest way to protect against the risks that you may not even know exist, is to demand a healthy discount to value of the security you are buying. Also called "margin of safety", a typical 30%-40% discount to the intrinsic value is a good protection against unknowns and your own mistakes in your analysis. In cases where the business has significant risks that are KNOWN, it may still be a terrific investment if you can buy the stock at a greater margin of safety. There are very few sure things in investing and the goal is to maximize your returns adjusted for risk. Sometimes, you may have to take some calculated risks when the potential rewards justify it. To protect your downside, a margin of safety approaching 80% or more may be required.

All this assumes that you are researching and analyzing the business of the company and its fundamentals before you make the buy decision. Not knowing the business, you are investing in exposes you to another type of risk. The stock may indeed be a great investment, but you may not be able to realize the profits if you miss the red flags that might appear in the future.

Risk is Not the Same as Volatility

If you have done your homework on your stock picks and are very confident in your research, and the company continues to execute in a way that affirms your thesis, why should you care if the stock price continues to go up or down on a daily basis. Daily stock fluctuations merely reflect the daily demand and supply of the shares, which for small cap stocks that are less liquid may be extreme. Have the patience to wait for the market to catch up with the value, which it will over time.

Volatility does create opportunities to increase your stake in the company. If the business is truly undervalued, any opportunity to increase ownership should be welcome.

On the flip side, it is quite possible that a stock may hit your valuation target on a short-term upswing. In cases like this, there is no reason to not liquidate your position if you can. Taking profits early is always better. You can redeploy your capital in other more undervalued assets. I always go in a new investment with a target sell price and put in a GTC limit order to sell at that price. Sometimes, I may revise the target price up or down depending on how the company performs in the future. This is not the same as a short-term speculation strategy. The difference is that you know what you are doing.

A disciplined buy and sell strategy and the commitment to stick with it is essential to manage your risk. It is altogether too easy to get carried away with "momentum" and "hype" when the stock price is on the rise. Emotions and sentiments should play no role in your investing.

With this being said, you should get in the habit of reading Wall Street's reports and ignoring their recommendations. More on this later!

BONUS #1: VALUE INVESTING – WHY DO YOU FAIL?

Value investors fail when they don't stay disciplined

Here is a riddle. Despite countless studies proving the superiority of value investing over growth or indexes, investors do not normally invest for value. Why is that? Don't they want better performance and greater wealth?

Christopher Browne of Tweedy, Browne in his presentation to the Columbia Business School (Nov 2000)[3] talks about how most money managers and investors are conditioned to track the benchmarks because of the one very basic human fear. The fear of standing out from the herd.

Browne also talks about various other behavioral tendencies people have that doom their aspirations to be a good value investor. For example, the urge to buy and sell when sitting still is normally more profitable. He cites a study of over 100,000

---

[3] VALUE INVESTING and BEHAVIORAL FINANCE Presentation by Christopher H. Browne to Columbia Business School Graham and Dodd Value Investing 2000 (on the web)

stock trades that found that for these investors, the stocks they sold on average outperformed the stocks they bought by 3.4% after a year. Ever thought "the stock always goes up after I sell". It is not always just in your mind!

You and most other investors are wired to make wrong decisions at critical times.

Even practicing value investors fail

Successful value investing requires 2 parts in equal measure: one of knowing the techniques to analyze stocks for value, and the second is the ability to stick to your discipline even when the market and overwhelming investor sentiment screams you are wrong.

Learning the valuation techniques is the easy part. Discipline is hard – it requires a process, patience, and the belief in the process. When you bet against the market as a value investor, you often stand alone. It takes courage to stick to your convictions.

For you will be tested. And often.

Over the last 15 years I have been investing for value, I have learned a few things I would like to share. Perhaps some of these may be unique to my philosophy.

1. **Buy for the deal, not for the stock price** – Most of the analysis I do is based on comparing market value to the intrinsic value. Using the absolute numbers, instead of the per share amounts helps in many ways. For example, it gives me a real feel for the business size and sales that can be compared to the industry. It also helps me remove the influences of such artificial constructs such as share repurchases or new issues. The stock price is pretty much the last thing I look at.
2. **When the deal gets better, buy more** – At one time, NEI stock was down about 40% after they announced future revenue declines due to EMC pulling their business away. However, the thesis for NEI was built on their strong balance sheet and as long as the company stayed profitable, the lower stock price was a much better deal than the price I initiated my position at. One should realize that the market is irrational in the short term and generally reacts to the extremes. I bought more as the stock price touched 40%-50% below the NCAV. Undervalued companies like this attract knowledgeable buyers and the company ended up being acquired, instantly flipping a 40% loss to a 15% gain.

3. **A stock may stay undervalued for a long time** – Nothing might happen for a long time, and then one fine day, the stock may get discovered. If the company is genuinely undervalued and is creating more value in the franchise through continued profits, it is calling out for attention that it is bound to get. One might get frustrated waiting for the stock to appreciate. Patience, and being able to do nothing at all when doing nothing is the best course of action is a key skill that very few investors possess.
4. **There is no hurry** – A corollary to being patient but in a different sort of way. If you are doing a due diligence on a stock and are not ready to make a definitive buy decision yet, do not buy. It does not matter if the stock suddenly caught on fire and you think the opportunity might slip away. There will be other ideas. Moving without conviction can be very expensive.
5. **Where is your guarantee?** – So, you think that the stock is undervalued and something or other might happen to unlock the value for you? Do you know what that "something or other" is that needs to happen? There are perhaps many different potential catalysts. What is the likelihood of one of these catalysts coming into play? How quickly? And how sure are you? In some cases, you may have a pretty good idea of the catalyst. In most cases however, these will be just different possibilities that you play around in your mind. Building these mental models before you buy the stock and refining them over time is not just wishful thinking. It helps you take any new data or development in the business and see which of these mental models it fits and that is where you find insights that 99% of the other investors will miss. Your guarantee of gain lies in the fact that 1) you get predisposed to looking for stocks where something good happening is more likely, and 2) you are in a better and more informed position to react when the time comes.

Most value investors fail one or several of these tests. Discipline is hard. Undervaluation does not always guarantee gains and you must know how and when they will come otherwise you are flying blind. And most value money managers feel compelled to stay fully invested even when it is not a good idea. Most of the success lies in how you approach investing, and independence from institutional constraints is very important.

Despite my calls for patience, it is important to realize that there are times action is required. How do you figure out when it is time to wait and when it is time to act? Experience helps, but more important is to have a well-defined process and strategy that you stick with. At times you will make wrong choices, but the beauty of having a process is that it can be refined with experience. What this does is to eliminate those simple mistakes that most investors make that little by little eat away their performance. Just doing this one simple thing statistically gives you an edge over most other investors over time.

BONUS #2: THINK VALUE INVESTING IS BUY AND HOLD INVESTING? THINK AGAIN

Value investing is a process that aims to deliver outstanding long-term returns. However, this should not be confused with the notion that value investors tend to buy and hold stocks for the long term. Buy and hold strategy ignores valuations over the holding period.

Many consider Warren Buffett as a great example of a successful value investor and Mr. Buffett does ask the question if he will be comfortable holding a company for decades before he decides on making an investment in the stock. However, this is merely to ensure that the company he is considering investing in has quality of earnings and a sustainable competitive advantage that will confer a level of safety should something unpredictable occur in the future. Please note that even Mr Buffett will exit a position quickly (or as quickly as the liquidity allows) if he determines that the investment no longer has a merit.

Value Investing is Essentially a Timing Exercise

It is not market timing in the sense most of us understand. Value investors choose to buy a stock when it is cheaper than the intrinsic value of the stock and sell it when it becomes more expensive. How is this different from market timing? Consider this hypothetical example.

A company can come out with a news that could not have been predicted. The same stock that was overvalued at a given price, may suddenly become undervalued AT THE SAME PRICE. A new joint venture, FDA approval when the expectation was more delays, striking gold, whatever. Reverse may be true as well. A value investor tries to "time" the value of the company, whereas a market timer will completely miss this development as it is not something he is concerned with.

It Gets Stranger: A Value Investor Might Sell a Stock that is Still Undervalued

The chief aim in value investing is to put as much distance between the stock price and the intrinsic value. Cheaper the stock price the better. Sometimes it happens that the investor might find a stock that is even greater value than the stocks he currently has in the portfolio. This new stock offers greater potential rewards at a greater margin of safety (meaning less risk). No value investor worth his salt will let this opportunity pass. If this means selling an existing holding that is relatively fully valued, then so be it.

Closely watch a value investors portfolio and you will find *stocks come in and stocks go out* quite frequently. At least more frequently then you will expect to see in a buy and hold portfolio. I have personally averaged 1-3 transactions per month in the last few months, but there have been months when not a single transaction was made and then there have been times when 4-5 transactions were done in a week. It all depends on the opportunities.

Is there a Place for Buy and Hold in a Value Investor's Portfolio?

Could be. There may be rare companies that continue to grow value at a rapid clip. These are the companies with a competitive moat. Still, the primary function of a value investor is efficient capital allocation, and short of tax considerations (especially for large capital gains), it is hard to make an argument for staying with an investment if a better opportunity exists.

FINAL THOUGHTS

By picking up this book, you have chosen to take the first step towards independent thinking about investments. This is a journey that can be very profitable and satisfying, but at the same time it will occasionally make you question your faith. After all, if you delegate the task of picking investments to a fund manager or an advisor, all you must do if the current one does not perform is to find a new one. But you know as well as anyone else, chasing performance does not work. A better way is to find out what adjustments need to be made to your own investment process and continuously improve them.

LEARN MORE ABOUT VALUE INVESTING AND HOW I CAN HELP YOU

- **Value Stock Guide Premium:** Explore our Premium membership program and receive my real-world portfolio you can use to model your investments directly. I provide you with deep research, recommendations to buy & sell including how much of your portfolio to allocate to a stock, and all risk management processes I employ. Also included is a periodic newsletter. Have questions or need to discuss a stock in the portfolio or want opinion on a stock you have been considering? You can do this in your member exclusive forum.

  Learn more at https://valuestockguide.com/membership/

- **Cut Down Your Stock Research Time by 80% (or more):** Stock Rover is a research platform built for fundamental investors. It has many pre-built value screens, as well as lets you build complex screens in a very intuitive way. Very affordable and supremely capable, this is the only tool I use in my research.

  Try it here https://valuestockguide.com/recommends/stock-rover/

ABOUT THE AUTHOR

Hi, my name is Shailesh Kumar. I have been investing using value investing principles for close to 20 years. My articles at Value Stock Guide are syndicated at Seeking Alpha, Trefis, Nasdaq.com, TalkMarkets.com and Investing.com. My articles have appeared on WealthFront, Forbes, Business Insider and many other sites and I have been featured on New York Times, US News and World Report, Huffington Post and CNBC.

My Background Summary

I am a private investor and entrepreneur. In the past I was a Management Consultant with AT Kearney, where I advised Fortune 100 companies with their strategic business issues. Later, I led finance at a fast growing AT Kearney incubated start up shaking up an old-school manufacturing sector in Midwest. After working as a CFO for the startup company, I later quit to pursue entrepreneurship. I acquired and managed steel service centers in SE Michigan which I ran for two years. Part of the story of my steel business is well recounted in this New York Times article. The bottom line is, I have seen and practiced all aspects of real business, as a manager, consultant to the senior executives, executive and a CEO. This has helped give me a perspective on business, both theoretical and practical, something very few analysts on the Wall Street possess. I rely on my business knowledge in evaluating my stocks and underlying business dynamics and the results have been just excellent. If you choose to invest with me, you get the use of my vast business experience to make wiser investment choices.

I have an MBA from University of Michigan and an undergraduate degree in Electrical Engineering.

How Can I Help You Grow Your Wealth?

So how does my e*xperience help me* pick stocks better? For one, I look at a business (and stock) from an owner's perspective. If the business is creating value for the owners (shareholders), it is a good investment at a right price. I do not worry about efficient markets or other academic theories – they often breakdown for the small capitalization stocks where I most often hunt for value. This allows me to focus on picking the right stocks and ignore the wall street noise.

Want to Build a Long-Term Value Portfolio Around My Recommendations?

I am a portfolio manager first. This means my primary consideration is managing and growing my own portfolio. I do not seek to maximize for the short term, and I do not chase short term fads. If you appreciate a disciplined long-term approach and a manager who has an excellent market beating track record, you should consider working with us. Learn more about our membership services

www.ingramcontent.com/pod-product-compliance
Lightning Source LLC
Chambersburg PA
CBHW030526220526
45463CB00007B/2739